# The Quotable Play Therapist:

## 238 of the All-Time Best Quotes on Play and Play Therapy

**Edited by
Charles Schaefer, Ph.D.
Heidi Kaduson, Ph.D.**

**JASON ARONSON INC.**
*Northvale, New Jersey*
*London*

This book was printed and bound by Haddon Craftsmen of Scranton, Pennsylvania.

**Library of Congress Cataloging-in-Publication Data**

The quotable play therapist : 238 of the all-time best quotes on play and play therapy / edited by Charles Schaefer, Heidi Kaduson.
     p. cm.
   Includes index.
   ISBN 1-56821-229-1
    1. Play therapy—Quotations, maxims, etc. 2. Play—Quotations, maxims, etc. 3. Recreation—Quotations, maxims, etc. I. Schaefer, Charles E. II. Kaduson, Heidi.
   [DNLM 1. Play and Playthings. 2. Aphorisms and Proverbs. 3. Leisure Activities. 4. Imagination—in infancy & childhood. 5. Laughter—in infancy & childhood. 6. Play Therapy—in infancy & childhood. 7. Child Development, WS 105.5.P5 Q9 1994]
RJ505.P6Q67  1994
155.4'18—dc20
DNLM/DLC
for Library of Congress                     94-371

Manufactured in the United States of America. Jason Aronson Inc. offers books and cassettes. For information and catalog write to Jason Aronson Inc., 230 Livingston Street, Northvale, New Jersey 07647.

# CHILD THERAPY SERIES

## A SERIES OF BOOKS EDITED BY
## CHARLES SCHAEFER

Cognitive-Behavioral Play Therapy
*Susan M. Knell*

Play Therapy in Action: A Casebook for Practitioners
*Terry Kottman and Charles Schaefer, Eds.*

Family Play Therapy
*Lois Carey and Charles Schaefer, Eds.*

The Quotable Play Therapist
*Charles Schaefer and Heidi Kaduson, Eds.*

Childhood Encopresis and Enuresis
*Charles Schaefer*

The Therapeutic Powers of Play
*Charles Schaefer, Ed.*

Play Therapy Techniques
*Donna Cangelosi and Charles Schaefer, Eds.*

Children in Residential Care: Critical Issues in Treatment
*Charles Schaefer and Arthur Swanson, Eds.*

Therapeutic Use of Child's Play
*Charles Schaefer, Ed.*

Clinical Handbook of Sleep Disorders in Children
*Charles Schaefer, Ed.*

Clinical Handbook of Anxiety Disorders in Children and
Adolescents
*Andrew R. Eisen, Christopher A. Kearney,
and Charles Schaefer, Eds.*

Understanding and Treating Fear and Anxiety in Children
and Adolescents: A Practitioner's Guide
*Andrew R. Eisen and Christopher Kearney*

# Contents

Introduction                                             vii

Section One:     The Nature of Play                        1

Section Two:     Symbolic Play/
                 Creative Imagination                     81

Section Three:   Humor/Laughter                          137

Section Four:    Games/Sport                             173

Section Five:    Playfulness/Youthfulness                197

Section Six:     Fun/Amusement                           211

Section Seven:   Relaxation/Stress
                 Reduction                               223

Section Eight:   Play Therapy                            239


Index of Authors                                         257

# Introduction

Historically our nation has not valued children's play. Our Puritan ancestors regarded the play of children as wasteful and at times even sinful. As a result, policies designed to contain or discourage children's play were established. The heritage of these policies and attitudes toward play persists today. There is a movement, for example, to stress academics and minimize play in early childhood education programs. Abstract pencil and paper worksheets are being emphasized in some schools at the expense of more interactive child-initiated play activities.

In order to be more effective advocates for play, we all can benefit from a clearer vision of what play can do for children and people of all ages. Over time, mankind's greatest thinkers have reflected on the value of play. This volume brings together for the first time a comprehensive collection of the accumulated wisdom on the meaning of play. In essence, the book is a celebration of the growth and healing powers of play.

In searching the available literature (current and historic) we sought quotations on play that could be called "great." By great we mean quotations that express important ideas in a brief but beautiful way. Included in this volume are ideas from scholars, philosophers, therapists, scientists, theologians, artists, and entertainers.

The quotations are grouped by category. The first and largest category contains quotations on the nature of play behavior itself. The other categories are Symbolic Play/Creative Imagination; Humor/Laughter; Games/Sport; Playfulness/Youthfulness; Fun/Amusement; Relaxation/Stress Reduction; and Play Therapy.

This book can never be complete because insights about the nature and value of play are ongoing. We invite readers to send additions and suggestions for new quotations so that this book may evolve and expand in coverage.

We hope you enjoy reading these quotations as much as we did collecting them, and that the wisdom contained in them will lead to a greater appreciation and use of the therapeutic powers of play.

Charles Schaefer
Heidi Kaduson
139 Temple Avenue
Hackensack, NJ 07601
January 1994

# Section One

## The Nature
## of Play

Play is a child's work and this is not a trivial pursuit.

— Alfred Adler

Play is the child's
response to life.

— Anonymous

In play, there is an
honesty, a frankness,
and a vividness in the
way children state
themselves.

— Virginia Axline

Play is a child's
natural medium for
self-expression.

— Virginia Axline

Enter into children's play and you will find the place where their minds, hearts, and souls meet.

— Virginia Axline

All work and no play
makes Jack a dull boy.

— John Bay

Play is a window on
cognitive development.

— Jay Belsky

Playing seems to be both disinterested and passionate at the same time; disinterested in that it is not for real, and passionate in the absorption it requires.

— Oliver Bevan

$\mathcal{P}$lay is the exultation
of the possible.

— Martin Buber

Play is basic to all normal, healthy children. It provides pleasure and learning and a minimum of risks and penalties for mistakes.

— Frank Caplan

Play has been man's
most useful preoccupa-
tion.

— Frank Caplan

The true object of
all human life is play.
Earth is the task
garden; heaven is a
playground.

— G. K. Chesterton

. . . in play, the ego
aspires to its full
expansion.

— E. Claparede

The understanding of play in childhood is an entering wedge into an epistemology that could release realization of the impulse toward self-transcendance as a survival function.

— Edith Cobb

Blessed be they who play for theirs is the Kingdom of Heaven.

— Emily Dickinson

Play is the beginning
of knowledge.

— George Dorsey

If A equals success, then the formula is A equals X plus Y plus Z. X is work. Y is play. Z is keep your mouth shut.

— Albert Einstein

Play is an expression of self-love because by means of it the individual looks after his or her own needs.

— David Elkind

It is a happy talent to know how to play.

— Ralph Waldo Emerson

There are toys for all ages.

— English Proverb

The most strenuous
and dangerous play is
by definition not work;
it does not produce
commodities.

— Erik Erikson

Child's play is the infantile form of the human ability to deal with experience by creating model situations and to master reality by experimenting and planning . . . no thinker can do more and no playing child less.

— Erik Erikson

$\mathbb{P}$lay is a function of
the ego, an attempt to
synchronize the bodily
and the social processes
with the self.

— Erik Erikson

The microsphere—
i. e., the small world of
manageable toys—is a
harbor which the child
establishes, to return to
when he needs to over-
haul his ego.

— Erik Erikson

Play is learning.

— JoAnn M. Farver

There is little that gives children greater pleasure than when a grown-up lets himself down to their level, renounces his oppressive superiority and plays with them as an equal.

— Sigmund Freud

As people grow up
they cease to play, and
they seem to give up
the yield of pleasure
which they gained from
playing.

— Sigmund Freud

$\mathcal{P}$lay appears in
children while they are
learning to make use
of words and to put
thoughts together.

— Sigmund Freud

Early childhood education is just that—education. The children are learning through play, forming the foundation for reading, math, self-esteem, and social skills that will come later on.

— Dana Friedman

Child's play is not
mere sport.  It is full
of meaning and serious
impact.  Cherish it and
encourage it.  For to
one who has insight
into human nature,
the trend of the whole
future life of the child
is revealed in his freely
chosen play.

— F. W. A. Froebel

Through the manipulation of toys, the child can show more adequately than through words how he feels about himself and the significant persons and events in his life.

— Haim Ginott

To play acknowl-
edges our humanity,
keeps the dark side
of the mind at bay,
initiates the child into
celebration, keeps the
sense of wonder alive
of those in later years
of life.

— Geoffrey Godbey

Play in a special physical and interpersonal environment can permit learning-disabled children to succeed and develop a feeling of satisfaction with themselves and their competencies.

— Louise F. Guerney

Play is the most essential category of human experience, the activity we constantly turn to without knowing it.

— James S. Hans

To read the language of play is to read the hearts and minds of children.

— Ruth Hartley

Man is most nearly
himself when he
achieves the serious-
ness of a child at play.

— Heraclitus

Whenever you trace
the origin of a skill
or practices which
played a crucial role in
the ascent of man, we
usually reach the realm
of play.

— Eric Hoffer

Play is a uniquely adaptive act, not subordinate to some other adaptive act, but with a special function of its own in human experience.

— Johan Huizinga

Play is a child's life
and the means by
which he comes to
understand the world
he lives in.

— Susan Isaacs

The discovery of the educational possibilities of the play side of life may be counted one of the greatest discoveries of the present day. It makes, I am convinced, the dawn of a new era in human education.

— L. P. Jacks

... all the beasts of
the field play.

— Job 40:20

When you're free,
you can play and when
you're playing, you
become free.

— Heidi Kaduson

The best way of getting to know children is by observing them play.

— Søren Kierkegaard

Play affords direct access to a child's unconscious. Play for the child is like free association for the adult.

— Melanie Klein

We can no longer afford to overlook this significant dimension in children's lives called "play," which affords such unique opportunities to view the inner world of childhood. We must look with wonder, search with intensity, and ponder with the patience of children. This activity is casually referred to as "play," for it is there that we will find the window to the child's world.

— Garry Landreth
— Lessie Perry

$\mathcal{P}$lay is a spontaneous and active process in which thinking, feeling, and doing can flourish since they are separated from the fear of failure or disastrous consequences.

— Linnet McMahon

The field of play is
where, to a large
extent, a sense of self
is generated.

— Russell Meares

We are playful mammals all our lives and that has been the reason for our remarkable adaptability and achievement as a species.

— Ashley Montagu

It should be noted that children at play are not playing about; their games should be seen as their most serious-minded activity.

— Montaigne

$P$erhaps the most
important family
interaction is play, for
family play promotes
the child's development
as a social being and a
sense of joy in living.

— Lisa Morris
— Linda Schulz

If I get to pick what I want to do, then it's play . . . if someone else tells me that I have to do it, then it's work.

— Patricia Nourot

In our play, we reveal
what kind of people we
are.

— Ovid

$\mathfrak{P}$lay is the only way
the highest intelligence
of humankind can
unfold.

— Joseph Chilton
Pearce

Play is in the service
of survival.

— Joseph Chilton
Pearce

Play is the universal characteristic in the young of all higher species.

— Joseph Chilton Pearce

We can be sure that all happenings, pleasant or unpleasant, in the child's life, will have repercussions on her dolls.

— Jean Piaget

$P$lay transforms
reality by assimilation
of reality to the needs
of the self.

— Jean Piaget

Our children from
their earliest years
must take part in all
the more lawful forms
of play, for if they are
not surrounded with
such an atmosphere
they can never grow up
to be well-conducted
and virtuous citizens.

— Plato

You can discover more about a person in an hour of play than in a year of conversation.

— Plato

What is the right
way of living?  Life
must be lived as play.

— Plato

Children need some-
one to reassure them
that play—their own,
unique, imaginative
play—is something to
be valued.

— Fred Rogers

Playing is a form
of relating and begins
very early when
parents start cuddling,
tickling and playing
with their infants.

— Theodore Isaac
Rubin

To the art of working well, a civilized race would add the art of playing well.

— George Santayana

We are never more
fully alive, more com-
pletely ourselves, or
more deeply engrossed
in anything than when
we are playing.

— Charles Schaefer

The child's tendency to play and replay past events or to anticipate future ones through imagery seems to be a basic capacity of the brain.

— Dorothy G. Singer

Play may be the main "business" of childhood, but if it's not fun it's not really play.

— Dorothy G. Singer

. . . play puts the child
into an active position
and converts felt depri-
vation into felt relief
and a sense of pleasur-
able gratification on a
make-believe basis. . . .

— A. J. Solnit

$O$n the seashore of
endless worlds, chil-
dren play.

— Rabindranath
Tagore

Work consists of whatever a body is obliged to do.  Play consists of whatever a body is not obliged to do.

— Mark Twain

You can do anything
with children if you
only play with them.

— Prince Otto
von Bismarck

Man plays only when he is in the full sense of the word a man, and he is only wholly man when he is playing.

— J. C. F. von Schiller

In play a child is always above his average age, above his daily behavior; in play, it is as though he were a head taller than himself.  As in the focus of a magnifying glass, play contains all developmental tendencies in a condensed form; in play, it is as though the child were trying to jump above the level of his normal behavior.

— L. S. Vygotsky

The creation of
voluntary intentions and
the formation of real-life
plans and volitional
motives—all appear in
play and make it the
highest level of preschool
development.

— L. S. Vygotsky

Children's propensity
to engage in that
extraordinary series of
behaviors characterized
as "play" is perhaps
the single great divid-
ing line between child-
hood and adulthood.

— Marie Winn

It is play that is universal, and that belongs to health.

— D. W. Winnicott

The thing about playing is always the precariousness of the interplay of personal psychic reality and the experience of control of actual objects.

— D. W. Winnicott

Cultural experience
begins with creative
living first manifested
in play.

— D. W. Winnicott

# Section Two

## Symbolic Play/ Creative Imagination

We have learned as common knowledge that much of the insensibility and hardness of the world is due to the lack of imagination which prevents a realization of the experiences of other people.

— Jane Addams

A toy is an escape to another reality!

— Anthea Alley

If one is lucky, a solitary fantasy can totally transform one million realities.

— Maya Angelou

Play is self-creation.

— E. James
Anthony

When family members
play make-believe games
together the structure
and contents of their
play expose covert layers
of their emotional inter-
relations. Observing
and analyzing such
games is like mentally
x-raying the family.

— Shlomo Ariel

I see the mind of a five-year-old as a volcano with two vents: destructiveness and creativeness.

— Sylvia Ashton-Warner

Imagination is the
highest kite that can
fly.

— Lauren Bacall

Demanding more
than the world can give
us, we require that
something be fabricated
to make up for the
world's deficiency.
This is only one exam-
ple of our demand for
illusions.

— Daniel J.
Boorstin

Childish fantasy, like
the sheath over the
bud, not only protects
but curbs the terrible
budding spirit, protects
not only innocence
from the world, but the
world from the power
of innocence.

— Elizabeth Bowen

The only truly happy
people are children and
the creative minority.

— Jean Caldwell

Play is the imposition of the imagination on the fabric of the real world; and can be achieved in terms of activity and manipulation of object and people or through imaginary solutions which can be shared with others.

— Theresa Caplan

The child's urge to "body forth the forms of things unknown" in the microcosm of child art and play bears a distinct resemblance to the morphogenesis characteristic of nature's long-term history, namely, evolution.

— Edith Cobb

The gift of fantasy
has meant more to me
than my talent for
absorbing positive
knowledge.

— Albert Einstein

Imagination is more important than knowledge.

— Albert Einstein

Indeed, some of their "working through" of fears by acting out or otherwise cognitively reinstating something that frightens them may succeed because it helps them represent that thing's benign reality while experiencing its scary appearance.

— J. H. Flavell

She has no imagina-
tion and that means no
compassion.

— Michael Foot

A toy car is a
projection of a real car,
made small enough for
a child's hand and
imagination to grasp.
A real car is a projection
of a toy car, made large
enough for an adult's
hand and imagination
to grasp.

— Michael Frayn

In play a child actively engages in an act of poetic creation wherein he creates a world that is self-pleasing.

— Sigmund Freud

The life of the boy has,
indeed, no purpose but that of
the outer representation of his
self; his life is, in truth, an
external representation of his
inner being, of his power,
particularly in and through
(plastic) material.

In the forms he fashions he does
not see outer forms which he is
to take in and understand; but
he sees in them the expression
of his spirit, of the laws and
activities of his own mind.

— F. W. A. Froebel

In play the child does what springs spontaneously from his mind and ear; here he is most nearly whole, self-directed, open and creative—and in this kind of situation he learns best.

— Robert M. Goldenson

Fantasies are more than substitutes for unpleasant reality; they are also dress rehearsals, plans. All acts performed in the world begin in the imagination.

— Barbara G. Harrison

The key to life is imagination. If you don't have that, no matter what you have, it's meaningless. If you do have imagination . . . you can make a feast of straw.

— Jane Stanton Hitchcock

No amount of skillful
invention can replace
the essential element of
imagination.

— Edward Hopper

Man, like Deity,
creates in his own
image.

— Elbert Hubbard

Symbolic play pro-
vides safe opportunities
for reenactment,
rehearsal, the practice
needed to strengthen
the child and prepare
him for dealing directly
with traumatizing
events.

— Beverly James

In the safe disguise of play, (the child) can balance power, reward himself with fabulous riches, vanquish those who do not do his bidding, and devour his enemies.

— Beverly James

Imagination is the
eye of the soul.

— Joseph Joubert

The dynamic principle of fantasy is play, which belongs also to the child, and as such it appears to be inconsistent with the principle of serious work. But without this playing with fantasy no creative work has ever yet come to birth. The debt we owe to the play of imagination is incalculable.

— Carl Jung

The creation of
something new is not
accomplished by the
intellect but by the
play instinct acting
from inner necessity.
The creative mind
plays with the objects
it loves.

— Carl Jung

As great scientists
have said and as all
children know, it is
above all by the imagi-
nation that we achieve
perception, and com-
passion, and hope.

— Ursula K.
     LeGuin

All children are artists
and it is an indictment
of our culture that so
many of them lose the
creativity, their unfet-
tered imagination, as
they grow older.

— Madeleine
    L'Engle

In play we can find
the roots of our adult
capacities to think
creatively and flexibly,
to innovate, adapt,
change.

— Ashley Montagu

$P$lay is the investiga-
tion, the involvement
of externals in one's
fantasy life.

— Mike Moore

Regarding fantasy as a mere escape from boredom and frustration is as one sided as the opposite view that we are driven to face reality only as a refuge from an inner life which is primary but terrifying. The balanced individual should not only have come to terms with both worlds but should, at times in his life, have been an active explorer in the sheer joy of exploration.

— T. Moore

Creative work is play. It is free speculation using the materials of one's chosen form.

— Stephen Nachmanovitch

— a sociocultural analysis of play must closely examine, rather than neglect, the central role of fantasy and imagination in play activity.

— Angeliki Nicolopoulou

Symbolic play helps
in the resolution of
conflicts and also in
the compensation of
unsatisfied needs.

— Jean Piaget

Every child is an
artist. The problem is
how to remain an artist
after growing up.

— Pablo Picasso

The world of reality
has its limits; the
world of imagination
is boundless.

— Jean-Jacques
Rousseau

The virtue of the imagination is its reaching, by intuition and intensity of gaze (not by reasoning, but by the authoritative opening and revealing power), a more essential truth than is seen at the surface of things.

— John Ruskin

In imagination, not in perception, lies the substance of experience, while knowledge and reason are but its chastened and ultimate form.

— George Santayana

Children are natural mythologists. They beg to be told tales and love not only to invent but to enact falsehoods.

— George Santayana

Making believe and pretending are among the wonders of the experience of being human.

— Dorothy G. Singer

Make-believe play is
an important means
by which the child can
begin to identify and
to try on for size the
varied and sometimes
confusing social roles
that characterize our
culture.

— Dorothy G.
Singer

Play gives children the opportunity to search for and experiment with alternative solutions to their problems.

— Jerome Singer

Imaginative play can make for a happy childhood.

— Jerome Singer

Research has shown that children who play often—both solitarily and socially—become more creative and imaginative than those whose exposure to play and toys is limited.

— Brian Sutton-Smith

When a child engages in imaginative play with a parent, a very special phenomenon is taking place: the child is generating and executing ideas based on its own experience in a context of mutual respect, interest and absence of criticism. Parent and child are free to experience each other in terms of possibilities. Constraints inherent in the usual roles they play in relation to each other may be temporarily put aside. The give and take of laughter and of shared "dangers" and "rescues" may enhance a positive sense of communion. Parents often have lost touch with their own childhood joys in fantasy play and can regain some of that excitement through play.

— R. B. Tower and
J. Singer

Play provides developing children with the means by which they can rehearse the experiences that matter in real life.

— Paul V. Trad

So you see, imagination needs moddling— long, inefficient, happy idling, dawdling and puttering.

— Brenda Ueland

Imagination and
fiction make up more
than three quarters of
our real life.

— Simone Weil

Most forms of human creativity have one aspect in common: the attempt to give some sense to the various impressions, emotions, experiences, and actions that fill our lives, and thereby to give some meaning and value to our existence. . . . The crisis of our time in the Western world is that the search for meaning has become meaningless for many of us.

— Victor Weisskopf

It is creative apper-
ception more than any-
thing else that makes
the individual feel that
life is worth living.

— D. W. Winnicott

It is by playing and only in playing that the individual child is able to be creative and to use the whole personality, and it is only in being creative that the individual discovers the self.

— D. W. Winnicott

# Section Three

## Humor/Laughter

If we consider the
frequent reliefs we
receive from laughter,
and how often it breaks
the gloom which is apt
to depress the mind,
one would take care
not to grow too wise
for so great a pleasure
of life.

— Joseph Addison

Laughter is the best medicine.

— Anonymous

He who laughs, lasts.

— Robert Anthony

Comedy is the saving grace which makes life bearable.

— S. N. Behrman

Laughter is the
corrective force which
prevents us from
becoming cranks.

— Henri Bergson

Humor is the short-
est distance between
two people.

— Victor Borge

Total absence of
humor renders life
impossible.

— Colette

Beasts can weep
when they suffer, but
they cannot laugh.

— John Dryden

Humor is one of God's most marvelous gifts. Humor gives us smiles, laughter, and gaiety. Humor reveals the roses and hides the thorns. Humor makes our heavy burdens light and smooths the rough spots in our pathways. Humor burdens us with the capacity to clarify the obscure, to simplify the complex, to deflate the pompous, to chastise the arrogant, to paint a moral, and to adorn a tale.

— Sam Ervin

Dreams serve predominantly for the avoidance of unpleasure, jokes for the attainment of pleasure; but all our mental activities converge in these two aims.

— Sigmund Freud

Jokes and witticisms
have the tendency
to bypass reality, to
provide relief from the
seriousness of life.

— Sigmund Freud

Once you get people
laughing, they're listen-
ing and you can teach
them almost anything.

— Herb Gardner

Humor is an affirmation of dignity, a declaration of man's superiority to all that befalls him.

— Romain Gary

Laughter is a tranquilizer with no side effects.

— Arnold Glasgow

Wit . . . is, after all,
a form of arousal.
We challenge one
another to be funnier
and smarter. It's high-
energy play. It's the
way friends make love
to one another.

— Anne Gottlieb

A keen sense of humor helps us to overlook the unbecoming, understand the unconventional, tolerate the unpleasant, overcome the unexpected, and outlast the unbearable.

— Billy Graham

It's no laughing matter,
but it doesn't matter if
you laugh.

— Jennie
Gudmundsen

Invite humor to be a
frequent visitor in your
home—but be sure you
laugh *with* not *at* each
other.

— Jane M. Healy

Life can be wildly
tragic at times, and
I've had my share.
But whatever happens
to you, you have to
keep a slightly comic
attitude.  In the final
analysis, you have got
not to forget to laugh.

— Katharine
    Hepburn

There is certainly no
defense against adverse
fortune which is, on
the whole, so effectual
as an habitual sense of
humor.

— T. W. Higginson

A man isn't poor if he can still laugh.

— Raymond Hitchcock

Having entertained wounded G.I.s in three wars, I have seen the healing power of laughter. Now science has confirmed that having fun—just feeling happy or joyous—has a measurable effect on our health and well-being.

— Bob Hope

If you don't learn to laugh at trouble, you won't have anything to laugh at when you grow old.

— Edgar Howe

At the height of laughter, the universe is flung into a kaleidoscope of new possibilities.

— Jean Houston

A laugh is worth a hundred groans in any market.

— Charles Lamb

As soon as you have made a thought, laugh at it.

— Lao-tzu

Laughter is by definition healthy.

— Doris Lessing

With the fearful
strain that is on me
night and day, if I did
not laugh I should die.

— Abraham Lincoln

She knew what all
smart women knew:
laughter made you live
better and longer.

— Gail Parent

I am persuaded that every time a man smiles, but much more when he laughs, it adds something to this fragment of life.

— Steine

A good laugh is sun-
shine in a house.

— William Makepeace
Thackeray

Laughter need not be
cut out of anything,
since it improves
everything.

— James Thurber

Wit is the only wall
between us and the
dark.

— Mark Van Doren

Funny is an attitude.

— Flip Wilson

# Section Four

## Games/Sport

The manner in which a child approaches a game, his choice and the importance he places on it, indicate his attitude and relationship to his environment and how he's related to his fellow man.

— Alfred Adler

A well-adjusted person is the one who can play bridge or golf as if they were games.

— Anonymous

There is an intensity
and a danger in football—
as in life generally—
which keeps us alive and
awake. It is a test of our
awareness and ability.
Like so much of life, it
presents us with the
choice of responding
either with fear or with
action and clarity.

— John Brodie

Football is, after all,
a wonderful way to get
rid of aggression with-
out going to jail for it.

— Heywood Hale
Broun

It's good for a child
to lose as well as win.
They must learn in life
they are going to be up
today and maybe down
tomorrow.

— Ruby Middleton
        Forsythe

If you watch a game, it's fun. If you play it, it's recreation. If you work at it, it's golf.

— Bob Hope

The spirit of playful competition is, as a social impulse, older than culture itself and pervades all life like a veritable ferment. Ritual grew up in sacred play; poetry was born in play and nourished on play; music and dancing were pure play. Wisdom and philosophy found expression in words and forms derived from religious contexts. The rules of warfare, the conventions of noble living were built on play-patterns. We have to conclude, therefore, that civilization is, in its earliest phases, played. It does not come from play like a babe detaching itself from the womb; it arises in and as play, and never leaves it.

— Johan Huizinga

Real civilization cannot exist in the absence of a certain play-element, for civilization presupposes limitation and mastery of the self, the ability not to confuse its own tendencies with the ultimate and highest goal, but to understand that it is enclosed within certain bounds freely accepted.

Civilization will, in a sense, always be played according to certain rules, and true civilization will always demand fair play.

— Johan Huizinga

I am sorry I have not learned to play at cards. It is very useful in life: it generates kindness and consolidates society.

— Samuel Johnson

Man is a gaming animal. He must always be trying to get the better in something or other.

— Charles Lamb

It is in games that
many men discover
their paradise.

— Robert Lynd

Pride in accomplishment is felt when you make a good play . . . in a game.

— Gwen Bailey Moore

Games dissolve many
learning problems.

— Gwen Bailey
Moore

Internationnal sport is
war without shooting.

— George Orwell

For when the One
  Great Scorer comes
To write against your
  name,
He marks—not that
  you won or lost—
But how you played
  the game.

— Grantland Rice

Football is good for the country. Every American has that feeling inside him that he'd like to hit someone. He can't do it in this kind of society. But he comes out to the ballpark and he's almost in the game. It keeps him from going soft. It's the fans' way of fighting for the country.

— Tom Roussel

Play is where the
action is and where
you test your character
out against objects or
opponents.

— Brian
Sutton-Smith

Most sorts of diversion in men, children, and other animals, are an imitation of fighting.

— Jonathan Swift

Golf is a good walk
spoiled.

— Mark Twain

Did you know,
throughout the cosmos
they found intelligent
life forms that play to
play?  We are the only
ones that play  to win.
Explains why we have
more than our share of
losers.

— Jane Wagner

Greater female sports participation is going to make stronger, more powerful women with a clearer sense of capabilities.

— Ellen Wahl

# Section Five

## Playfulness/
## Youthfulness

I used to do whatever I felt like doing—it didn't have to do with whether it was important for the development of nuclear physics, but whether it was interesting and amusing to play with. . . . So I got this new attitude. Now that I am burned . . . I am going to *play* with physics, whenever I want to, without worrying about any importance whatsoever . . . just doing it for the fun of it. And before I knew it . . . I was "playing"—working really—and with the same old problem I loved so much. . . . It was effortless. It was easy to play with these things. It was like uncorking a bottle. There was no importance to what I was doing, but ultimately there were the diagrams and the whole business that I got the Nobel prize for came from the piddling around with the wobbling plate.

— Richard Feynman

A grownup is a
child with layers on.

— Woody Harrelson

For real playing,
man, as long as he
plays, must be a child
again.

— Johan Huizinga

The aging process
has you firmly in its
grasp if you never get
the urge to throw a
snowball.

— Doug Larson

Play is what I do
for a living; the work
comes in evaluating the
results of the play.

— Mac MacDougall

The wise man retains his childhood habit of mind.

— Mencius

Adults are nothing
more than deteriorated
children.

— Ashley Montagu

In every real man a
child is hidden who
wants to play.

— Friedrich Wilhelm
Nietzsche

We don't stop playing because we grow old; we grow old because we stop playing.

— George Bernard Shaw

We become old when we neglect the child in us who wants to play.

— George Bernard Shaw

The person who gets in touch with her or his own playfulness, imaginative resources and childhood joys is much more likely to offer the child richer opportunities for development than the adult who merely provides good physical care, and even love, for the child without exposing him to the whimsy and joy of make-believe.

— Dorothy G. Singer

Life is too important
to be taken seriously.

— Oscar Wilde

# Section Six

## Fun/
## Amusement

A company that has fun, where employees lunch with each other, put cartoons on the wall and celebrate, is spirited, creative, and usually profitable.

— David Baum

An ounce of mirth
is worth a pound of
sorrow.

— Richard Baxter

The first service a
child doth his father is
to make him foolish.

— George Herbert

If man insisted always on being serious, and never allowed himself a bit of fun and relaxation, he would go mad or become unstable without knowing it.

— Herodotus

Everything I have
ever done I have done
for the fun of it.

— Irving Langmuir

Of middle age the best that can be said is that a middle-aged person has likely learned how to have a little fun in spite of his troubles.

— Don Marquis

One would be in less danger
from the wiles of the stranger,
if one's own kin and kith
were more fun to be with.

— Ogden Nash

Let early education be
a sort of amusement.

— Plato

A merry heart doeth
good like a medicine.

— Proverbs 17:22

Frame your mind to mirth and merriment, which bars a thousand harms and lengthens life.

— William Shakespeare

# Section Seven

## Relaxation/ Stress Reduction

$\mathcal{P}$lay so that you may
be serious.

— $\mathcal{A}$nacharsis

Play may be viewed as a device for regulating the level of emotional arousal around sensitive, emotionally laden themes in the child's psyche.

— Shlomo Ariel

Play is young chil-
dren's only defense
against the many real
or imagined attacks and
slights they encounter.

— David Elkind

$\mathcal{P}$lay is nature's way
of dealing with stress
for children as well as
adults.

— David Elkind

Choose such pleasures as recreate much and cost little.

— Thomas Fuller

The work ethic has
spun way out of control.
In earlier eras, there were
natural periods of down-
time due to the seasons
during which people
couldn't plant or harvest
crops. But now there's
no limit to the amount
of work we can do.

— Geoffrey Godbey

$\mathcal{P}$lay could preserve
sanity by preventing a
dangerous pile-up of
too much feeling.

— $\mathcal{R}$uth $\mathcal{H}$artley

Relaxation and enjoyment of spontaneous activities facilitates creative thinking.

— Jane M. Healy

Do not take life too
seriously.  You will
never get out of it
alive.

— Elbert Hubbard

Our minds need relaxation
and give way
Unless we mix with work
a little play

— Molière

When one occupies
the conscious, volitional
self in relaxed, nonpur-
posive play, this gets the
anxious, tightly screen-
ing volitional self out of
the way, freeing the vast
computational abilities
of the brain.

— Joseph Chilton
Pearce

One of the primary values of play may be its capacity to alleviate emotional distress and consequently allow the child to master and achieve the skills needed to regulate distress in real life.

— Paul V. Trad

Through play reality
loses its seriousness.

— J. C. F.
von Schiller

# Section Eight

## Play Therapy

Laughter is the best
therapy.

— Anonymous

Young patients talk more freely, spontaneously and less defensively in the language of play since they seem to regard this special realm, preconsciously, as once removed from the pressures and demands of everyday life.

— J. Anthony

$\mathcal{P}$lay therapy experience is an emotional
experience that brings
about reorganization of
meanings, concepts,
feelings, self-under-
standing.

— Virginia Axline

Play therapy has
become the main avenue
for helping young
children with their
emotional difficulties.

— Bruno Bettelheim

To play it out is the most natural auto-therapeutic measure childhood affords.

— Erik Erikson

Modern play therapy is based on the observation that a child made insecure by a secret hate or fear of the natural protectors of his play in the family and neighborhood seems able to use the protective sanction of an understanding adult to regain some play peace. Grandmothers and favorite aunts may have played that role in the past; its professional elaboration of today is the play therapist. The most obvious condition is that the child has the toys and adult for himself, and that sibling rivalry, parental nagging, or any kind of sudden interruption does not disturb the unfolding of his play intentions.

— Erik Erikson

When the clinician uses a playful therapy style, the child not only gets great benefit from the message that he is a fun kid to be with, but also learns play-skills that often need to be part of the treatment plan.

— Beverly James

Play therapy has grown out of attempts to provide the child an avenue for growth using his most natural language, play.

— Dessie Oliver James

Play therapy is a relationship between the child and therapist in the setting of the playroom, where the child is encouraged to express himself freely, to release pent-up emotions and repressed feelings, and to work through his fear and anger so that he comes to be himself and functions in terms of his real potentials and abilities.

— Clark E. Moustakas

Play therapy is a
time when the thera-
pist in all genuineness
tries to see and under-
stand the world exactly
as the child views it.

— Carl R. Rogers

The modern profession of play therapy finds its roots in a long and global tradition of the use of play to promote psychological development and well-being in people of all ages.

— Charles Schaefer

$P$lay therapy has a long past, but only a short history.

— Charles Schaefer

From our work we know that people are half over their emotional problems once they manage to laugh at their predicament.

— Paul Watzlawick

Playing is itself a
therapy.

— D. W. Winnicott

**P**sychotherapy is done in the overlap of the two play areas, that of the patient and that of the therapist.

— D. W. Winnicott

# Index

| | |
|---|---|
| Addams, J. | 83 |
| Addison, J. | 139 |
| Adler, A. | 3, 175 |
| Alley, A. | 84 |
| Anacharsis | 225 |
| Angelou, M. | 85 |
| Anonymous | 4, 140, 176, 241 |
| Anthony, E. J. | 86 |
| Anthony, J. | 242 |
| Anthony, R. | 141 |
| Ariel, S. | 87, 226 |
| Ashton-Warner, S. | 88 |
| Axline, V. | 5, 6, 7, 243 |
| | |
| Bacall, L. | 89 |
| Baum, D. | 213 |
| Baxter, R. | 214 |
| Bay, J. | 8 |
| Behrman, S. N. | 142 |
| Belsky, J. | 9 |
| Bergson, H. | 143 |
| Bettelheim, B. | 244 |
| Bevan, O. | 10 |

| | |
|---|---|
| Boorstin, D. | 90 |
| Borge, V. | 144 |
| Bowen, E. | 91 |
| Brodie, J. | 177 |
| Broun, H. H. | 178 |
| Buber, M. | 11 |
| | |
| Caldwell, J. | 92 |
| Caplan, F. | 12, 13 |
| Caplan, T. | 93 |
| Chesterton, G. K. | 14 |
| Claparede, E. | 15 |
| Cobb, E. | 16, 94 |
| Colette | 145 |
| | |
| Dickinson, E. | 17 |
| Dorsey, G. | 18 |
| Dryden, J. | 146 |
| | |
| Einstein, A. | 19, 95, 96 |
| Elkind, D. | 20, 227, 228 |
| Emerson, R. W. | 21 |
| English Proverb | 22 |
| Erikson, E. | 23, 24, 25, 26, 245, 246 |
| Ervin, S. | 147 |

| | |
|---|---|
| Farver, J. M. | 27 |
| Feynman, R. | 199 |
| Flavell, J. H. | 97 |
| Foot, M. | 98 |
| Forsythe, R. M. | 179 |
| Frayn, M. | 99 |
| Freud, S. | 28, 29, 30, 100, 148, 149 |
| Friedman, D. | 31 |
| Froebel, F. W. A. | 32, 101 |
| Fuller, T. | 229 |
| | |
| Gardner, H. | 150 |
| Gary, R. | 151 |
| Ginott, H. | 33 |
| Glasgow, A. | 152 |
| Godbey, G. | 34, 230 |
| Goldenson, R. M. | 102 |
| Gottlieb, A. | 153 |
| Graham, B. | 154 |
| Gudmundsen, J. | 155 |
| Guerney, L. F. | 35 |
| | |
| Hans, J. S. | 36 |
| Harrelson, W. | 200 |
| Harrison, B. G. | 103 |

Hartley, R.                          37, 231
Healy, J.                           156, 232
Hepburn, K.                             157
Heraclitus                               38
Herbert, G.                             215
Herodotus                               216
Higginson, T. W.                        158
Hitchcock, J. S.                        104
Hitchcock, R.                           159
Hoffer, E.                               39
Hope, B.                           160, 180
Hopper, E.                              105
Houston, J.                             162
Howe, E.                                161
Hubbard, E.                        106, 233
Huizinga, J.            40, 181, 182, 201

Isaacs, S.                               41

Jacks, L. P.                             42
James, B.                     107, 108, 247
James, D. O.                            248
Job                                      43
Johnson, S.                             183
Joubert, J.                             109
Jung, C.                           110, 111

Kaduson, H.                 44
Kierkegaard, S.             45
Klein, M.                   46

Lamb, C.               163, 184
Landreth, G.                47
Langmuir, I.               217
Lao-tzu                    164
Larson, D.                 202
LeGuin, U. K.              112
L'Engle, M.                113
Lessing, D.                165
Lincoln, A.                166
Lynd, R.                   185

MacDougall, M.             203
Marguis, D.                218
McMahon, L.                 48
Meares, R.                  49
Mencius                    204
Molière                    234
Montagu, A.        50, 114, 205
Montaigne                   51
Moore, G. B.           186, 187
Moore, M.                  115
Moore, T.                  116

Morris, L.     52
Moustakas, C. E.     249

Nachmanovitch, S.     117
Nash, O.     219
Nicolopoulou, A.     118
Nietzche, F. W.     206
Nourot, P.     53

Orwell, G.     188
Ovid     54

Parent, G.     167
Pearce, J. C.     55, 56, 57, 235
Perry, L.     47
Piaget, J.     58, 59, 119
Picasso, P.     120
Plato     60, 61, 62, 220
Proverbs     221

Rice, G.     189
Rogers, C. R.     250
Rogers, F.     63
Rousseau, J-J.     121
Roussel, T.     190
Rubin, T. I.     64

| | |
|---|---|
| Ruskin, J. | 122 |
| | |
| Santayana, G. | 65, 123, 124 |
| Schaefer, C. | 66, 251, 252 |
| Schulz, L. | 52 |
| Shakespeare, W. | 222 |
| Shaw, G. B. | 207, 208 |
| Singer, D. G. | 67, 68, 125, 126, 209 |
| Singer, J. | 127, 128, 130 |
| Solnit, A. J. | 69 |
| Steine | 168 |
| Sutton-Smith, B. | 129, 191 |
| Swift, J. | 192 |
| | |
| Tagore, R. | 70 |
| Thackeray, W. M. | 169 |
| Thurber, J. | 170 |
| Tower, R. B. | 130 |
| Trad, P. V. | 131, 236 |
| Twain, M. | 71, 193 |
| | |
| Ueland, B. | 132 |
| | |
| Van Doren, M. | 171 |
| von Bismarck, Prince O. | 72 |
| von Schiller, J. C. F. | 73, 237 |

Vygotsky, L. S.                74, 75

Wagner, J.                       194
Wahle, E.                        195
Watzlawick, P.                   253
Weil, S.                         133
Weisskopf, V.                    134
Wilde, O.                        210
Wilson, F.                       172
Winn, M.                          76
Winnicott, D. W.      77, 78, 79, 135,
                         136, 254, 255